HEAVY DUTY, LESS TIME MORE GAINS

G.P. Manso

DEDICATION

Dear Family and Friends of the Gym,

It is with great pleasure that I dedicate my book on the Heavy Duty training system to all of you. Your unwavering support and encouragement have been instrumental in helping me achieve my fitness goals, and I am grateful for your presence in my life.

This book is a testament to our shared passion for health and fitness, and I hope that it will serve as a valuable resource to all of you on your own fitness journeys. Whether you're a seasoned athlete or just starting out, the Heavy Duty training system outlined in these pages can help you reach new levels of strength, endurance, and overall fitness.

I want to thank each and every one of you for being a part of my life, both inside and outside of the gym. Your friendship and camaraderie have been a source of motivation and inspiration, and I am honored to share this book with you.

To my family, I am grateful for your unconditional love and support. Your belief in me has never wavered, and I am lucky to have you in my corner.

To my friends of the gym, thank you for pushing me to be my best self. Our shared experiences in the gym have created a bond that extends far beyond the walls of the weight room, and I am thankful for each and every one of you.

This book is dedicated to all of you, and I hope that it inspires you to reach new heights in your fitness journey.

With gratitude and appreciation,

CONTENTS

ACKNOWLEDGMENTS

Writing a book is never a solitary endeavor, and I have been fortunate to have the support and assistance of many people throughout this process. I would like to express my heartfelt thanks to the following individuals:

First and foremost, I would like to thank my family for their unwavering support and encouragement throughout the writing of this book. Their love and understanding have been essential to my success, and I am grateful for their constant presence in my life.

I would also like to express my deep gratitude to my friends of the gym, who have been a source of inspiration and motivation throughout my fitness journey. Your camaraderie and shared experiences have shaped me into the athlete and writer that I am today.

My editor and publisher have been invaluable in bringing this book to fruition. Their guidance and expertise have been essential to the success of this project, and I am grateful for their dedication and professionalism.

Finally, I want to acknowledge the many trainers, athletes, and researchers whose work has informed and inspired the Heavy Duty training system. Their contributions to the field of fitness have been instrumental in shaping my own training philosophy, and I am honored to be a part of this community.

Thank you to all of you for your support and encouragement. Without you, this book would not have been possible.

Sincerely,

1 INTRODUCTION TO HEAVY DUTY TRAINING

In this chapter, we'll introduce the concept of Heavy Duty Training and provide an overview of the method. Heavy Duty Training is a style of resistance training that emphasizes high-intensity workouts with fewer exercises, sets, and repetitions than traditional bodybuilding programs. The goal is to maximize muscle fiber stimulation and minimize the risk of injury by performing exercises with the highest possible level of intensity.

The Heavy Duty Training method was popularized by a number of well-known bodybuilders, including Mike Mentzer and Dorian Yates. Both of these athletes used Heavy Duty Training to great effect during their competitive careers and continue to promote the method to this day.

Mike Mentzer was a champion bodybuilder in the 1970s and 1980s who trained with the legendary Arthur Jones, the founder of Nautilus exercise equipment. Mentzer believed that traditional bodybuilding programs were inefficient and advocated for a more intense, lower-volume approach to training. He developed a system of training that involved performing just one set per exercise, using a weight that could be lifted to failure in 8-12 repetitions. Mentzer's approach was controversial at the time but has since been embraced by many athletes and trainers.

Dorian Yates is another well-known bodybuilder who used Heavy Duty Training to great effect. He won six consecutive Mr. Olympia titles from 1992-1997 and is widely regarded as one of the greatest bodybuilders of all time. Yates trained with a similar approach to Mentzer, performing just one set per exercise with a high level of intensity.

In this chapter, we'll explore the principles that underpin Heavy Duty

Training and how they differ from traditional bodybuilding programs. We'll also discuss the benefits of Heavy Duty Training, including increased muscle fiber recruitment, reduced risk of injury, and faster recovery times.

Overall, this chapter will provide readers with a solid understanding of what Heavy Duty Training is and why it's an effective approach to building muscle. By the end of the chapter, readers will have a clear idea of what to expect from the rest of the book and how to apply the principles of Heavy Duty Training to their own workouts.

To fully understand Heavy Duty Training, it's important to first understand the concept of intensity. Intensity is a measure of how much weight you're lifting in relation to your maximum strength. The higher the intensity, the more muscle fibers you're recruiting and the greater the stimulus for muscle growth.

Traditional bodybuilding programs typically involve high volume, meaning more sets and repetitions, and lower intensity. While this approach can be effective for some, it can also lead to overtraining and injury, as well as a plateau in muscle growth.

Heavy Duty Training, on the other hand, involves fewer exercises, sets, and repetitions but with a much higher level of intensity. This means that you're lifting closer to your maximum strength, which stimulates a greater number of muscle fibers and results in faster gains.

The key to Heavy Duty Training is to lift until failure. This means performing each set with a weight that you can lift for only a certain number of repetitions before reaching muscle failure, or the point where you can no longer complete another repetition with good form. By pushing your muscles to failure, you're ensuring that you're recruiting as many muscle fibers as possible and sending a strong signal to your body to grow and adapt.

Another important principle of Heavy Duty Training is progression. As you become stronger and more experienced, you'll need to continually challenge your muscles to avoid plateauing. This can be done by increasing the weight, using intensity techniques such as forced reps or drop sets, or reducing rest periods between sets.

Heavy Duty Training has been shown to be an effective method for building muscle, with many athletes and bodybuilders achieving impressive results. However, it's not a one-size-fits-all approach and may not be suitable for everyone. It's important to listen to your body and adapt the training program to suit your own goals and abilities.

In the next chapter, we'll dive deeper into the principles of Heavy Duty Training and provide guidance on how to design an effective workout program using this method.

2 THE PRINCIPLES OF HEAVY DUTY TRAINING

In this chapter, we'll explore the scientific principles behind Heavy Duty Training and why it's such an effective method for building muscle.

At the heart of Heavy Duty Training is the principle of progressive overload. This principle states that in order to build muscle, you need to continually increase the demand placed on your muscles over time. This can be done by increasing the weight you lift, the number of repetitions you perform, or the intensity of your workouts.

Another important principle of Heavy Duty Training is muscle fiber recruitment. The goal is to stimulate as many muscle fibers as possible in each exercise, which can be achieved through high-intensity, low-volume workouts. By lifting heavy weights to failure, you're forcing your muscles to recruit a higher percentage of muscle fibers than with lighter weights and higher reps.

In addition, Heavy Duty Training emphasizes proper form and technique to ensure that you're targeting the intended muscle group and reducing the risk of injury. This means using a slow and controlled lifting tempo, avoiding momentum or cheating, and focusing on the mind-muscle connection to really feel the muscle working.

Rest and recovery are also key principles of Heavy Duty Training. Because you're pushing your muscles to the limit with each workout, it's important to give them adequate time to recover and rebuild. This means taking at least one day of rest between workouts and allowing for longer rest periods between sets.

Finally, Heavy Duty Training emphasizes the importance of tracking your progress over time. By keeping a record of your workouts and tracking your lifts and repetitions, you can see how your strength and muscle mass are improving over time. This can also help you identify areas for improvement and adjust your workouts accordingly.

By understanding and applying these principles of Heavy Duty Training, you can design an effective workout program that maximizes muscle fiber recruitment, stimulates growth, and minimizes the risk of injury. In the next chapter, we'll provide guidance on how to apply these principles to your own training program and create a workout plan that works for you.

Another important principle of Heavy Duty Training is the concept of muscular failure. In traditional bodybuilding programs, athletes typically perform sets of 8-12 reps and stop when they feel like they can no longer perform the exercise with proper form. However, in Heavy Duty Training, the goal is to push your muscles to the point of failure, which means you can no longer perform the exercise with good form and control.

By pushing your muscles to failure, you're signaling to your body that it needs to adapt and grow stronger in order to handle the demands you're placing on it. This can result in greater muscle fiber recruitment and growth, as well as improvements in overall strength and fitness.

Another key element of Heavy Duty Training is the use of low-volume workouts. Unlike traditional bodybuilding programs that may involve performing multiple sets of each exercise, Heavy Duty Training typically involves performing just one or two sets per exercise. This allows you to focus your energy and effort on each set, lifting with maximum intensity and effort.

The intensity of each set is also a critical aspect of Heavy Duty Training. Rather than focusing on the number of reps or sets, the goal is to lift as heavy as possible with good form and control, and to push yourself to failure on each set. This can help to maximize muscle fiber recruitment and stimulate growth, while also minimizing the amount of time you need to spend in the gym.

Finally, Heavy Duty Training emphasizes the importance of adequate rest and recovery. Because you're pushing your muscles to the limit with each workout, it's important to give them time to recover and rebuild. This means taking at least one day of rest between workouts and allowing for longer rest periods between sets.

Overall, the principles of Heavy Duty Training emphasize the importance of training with high intensity, low volume, and proper form and technique. By focusing on these principles, you can create a workout program that is both efficient and effective for building muscle, strength, and overall fitness.

In addition to the principles of muscular failure, low-volume workouts, and high intensity, Heavy Duty Training also places a great deal of importance on proper form and technique. Lifting with good form is crucial not only for maximizing muscle growth and strength, but also for reducing the risk of injury.

Proper form involves maintaining a neutral spine, engaging the core, and using controlled, deliberate movements. It's important to lift with a full range of motion, taking the muscle through both the concentric and eccentric phases of the movement.

To ensure proper form and technique, it's often helpful to have a coach or training partner who can provide feedback and guidance. They can help you to identify areas where you may be compensating or using poor form, and offer suggestions for how to correct these issues.

Another important aspect of Heavy Duty Training is the use of periodization. Periodization involves breaking up your training program into distinct phases, each with its own specific goals and training parameters.

For example, a periodized Heavy Duty Training program might involve several weeks of high-volume, low-intensity training followed by several weeks of low-volume, high-intensity training. This can help to prevent plateaus, keep your body guessing, and ensure continued progress over time.

Finally, it's important to listen to your body and make adjustments to your training program as needed. While Heavy Duty Training can be highly effective for building muscle and strength, it's also a demanding form of training that requires careful attention to recovery and nutrition.

If you find that you're consistently fatigued or experiencing pain or discomfort, it may be a sign that you need to adjust your training program or take additional rest days. Similarly, if you're not seeing the progress you'd like, it may be time to increase the intensity or volume of your workouts.

By incorporating these principles into your Heavy Duty Training program, you can create a highly effective and efficient workout routine that maximizes muscle growth, strength, and overall fitness. In the next chapter, we'll provide specific examples of Heavy Duty Training workouts and programming options.

3 DESIGNING A HEAVY DUTY TRAINING PROGRAM

Now that we've explored the principles behind Heavy Duty Training, let's dive into how to design an effective program using this method.

The first step is to choose the right exercises. Heavy Duty Training typically involves compound exercises that work multiple muscle groups at once, such as squats, deadlifts, bench press, and pull-ups. These exercises allow you to lift heavy weights and recruit a large number of muscle fibers, which is crucial for maximizing growth.

Next, you'll need to determine your training frequency. Heavy Duty Training typically involves fewer workouts per week than traditional bodybuilding programs, with many athletes and bodybuilders training just two to four days per week. This allows for more time for rest and recovery between workouts, which is important for muscle growth.

Once you've determined your training frequency, it's important to set your training volume. Because Heavy Duty Training involves lifting heavy weights to failure, the volume of each workout is typically lower than with traditional bodybuilding programs. This means fewer sets and reps per exercise, but with higher intensity.

To ensure progressive overload, it's important to track your lifts and strive to increase the weight or repetitions over time. This can be done by increasing the weight by a small amount each workout or using intensity techniques such as forced reps or drop sets to push your muscles to their limits.

Rest and recovery are also crucial to a successful Heavy Duty Training program. Because you're lifting heavy weights to failure, your muscles will need adequate time to recover and rebuild. This means taking at least one day of rest between workouts and allowing for longer rest periods between sets.

Finally, nutrition and supplementation play an important role in supporting muscle growth and recovery. Eating a diet rich in protein, carbohydrates, and healthy fats can provide your body with the nutrients it needs to build muscle. Supplements such as protein powder, creatine, and BCAAs can also help support muscle growth and recovery.

By following these guidelines for designing a Heavy Duty Training program, you can maximize muscle growth, strength, and overall fitness. However, it's important to listen to your body and adjust your program as needed to suit your own goals and abilities. In the next chapter, we'll provide specific workout examples and programming options for Heavy Duty Training.

One of the great benefits of Heavy Duty Training is its flexibility. Because the principles of the program can be applied to a wide range of exercises and training modalities, there are many different workout options to choose from.

In this chapter, we'll provide some examples of Heavy Duty Training workouts and programming options to help you get started. Remember, the key to success with Heavy Duty Training is to focus on high intensity, low volume, and proper form and technique.

Example 1: Full Body Heavy Duty Workout

This workout involves performing one or two sets of each exercise, lifting to failure on each set. Rest for at least one minute between sets and exercises.

Squats
Bench press
Deadlifts
Pull-ups
Dumbbell shoulder press
Barbell curls
Tricep extensions
Calf raises
Example 2: Upper/Lower Split Heavy Duty Workout

This workout splits the body into upper and lower sections, with a focus on compound exercises that work multiple muscle groups at once. Perform one or two sets of each exercise, lifting to failure on each set. Rest for at least one minute between sets and exercises.

Upper Body:

Bench press
Pull-ups
Dumbbell shoulder press
Barbell curls
Tricep extensions
Lower Body:

Squats
Deadlifts
Leg press
Calf raises
Example 3: Heavy Duty Training with Machines

Heavy Duty Training can also be performed using weight machines, which can be especially helpful for beginners or those with limited mobility. Perform one or two sets of each exercise, lifting to failure on each set. Rest for at least one minute between sets and exercises.

Leg press machine
Chest press machine
Lat pull-down machine
Shoulder press machine
Bicep curl machine
Tricep extension machine
Leg curl machine
Calf raise machine
These are just a few examples of the many Heavy Duty Training workout options available. Remember to focus on high intensity, low volume, and proper form and technique, and to incorporate rest and recovery into your routine. With consistency and dedication, you can achieve impressive muscle growth and strength gains through Heavy Duty Training.

Example 4: Push/Pull Heavy Duty Workout

This workout splits the body into push and pull sections, with a focus on compound exercises that work multiple muscle groups at once. Perform one or two sets of each exercise, lifting to failure on each set. Rest for at least one minute between sets and exercises.

Push:

Bench press
Dumbbell shoulder press
Tricep extensions
Chest flyes
Pull:

Pull-ups
Barbell curls
Lat pull-downs
Seated rows
Example 5: Heavy Duty Training for Legs

This workout focuses on building strength and size in the legs, with a combination of compound and isolation exercises. Perform one or two sets of each exercise, lifting to failure on each set. Rest for at least one minute between sets and exercises.

Squats
Deadlifts
Leg press
Leg extensions
Leg curls
Calf raises
Example 6: Heavy Duty Training for Chest and Arms

This workout targets the chest and arms, with a focus on compound exercises for the chest and isolation exercises for the arms. Perform one or two sets of each exercise, lifting to failure on each set. Rest for at least one minute between sets and exercises.

Bench press
Incline bench press
Chest flyes
Barbell curls
Dumbbell curls
Hammer curls
Tricep pushdowns
Overhead tricep extensions
Remember, these workouts are just examples, and you can customize your

own Heavy Duty Training program to fit your individual needs and goals. Incorporate the principles of high intensity, low volume, and proper form and technique, and adjust your program as needed to ensure continued progress over time.

4 NUTRITION FOR HEAVY DUTY TRAINING

Proper nutrition is a key component of any muscle-building program, and Heavy Duty Training is no exception. In order to maximize your results, it's important to fuel your body with the nutrients it needs to build and repair muscle tissue, as well as to support overall health and wellness.

Here are some nutrition tips to keep in mind when following a Heavy Duty Training program:

Eat enough calories: In order to build muscle, you need to be in a calorie surplus, meaning you consume more calories than you burn. Aim to consume an extra 250-500 calories per day above your maintenance level to support muscle growth.

Focus on protein: Protein is essential for building and repairing muscle tissue. Aim to consume 1-1.5 grams of protein per pound of body weight per day, and include high-quality sources such as lean meats, poultry, fish, eggs, and plant-based options like tofu, tempeh, and legumes.

Don't neglect carbs and fats: While protein is important, don't overlook the importance of carbohydrates and fats in your diet. Carbs provide energy for your workouts, while healthy fats support hormone production and overall health. Aim to consume a balance of all three macronutrients.

Hydrate properly: Adequate hydration is important for muscle function and recovery. Aim to drink at least half your body weight in ounces of water each day, and more if you are sweating heavily during your workouts.

Consider supplementation: While a healthy diet should be the foundation of your nutrition plan, certain supplements may help support muscle growth and recovery. Consider adding protein powder, creatine, and/or branched-chain amino acids (BCAAs) to your regimen.

Remember, nutrition is highly individualized, and what works for one person may not work for another. Experiment with different approaches to find what works best for you, and consult with a registered dietitian or nutritionist if you need additional guidance. With a proper nutrition plan, you can support your Heavy Duty Training program and maximize your muscle-building potential.

Time your meals properly: To optimize muscle growth, aim to consume protein and carbs within 30 minutes to an hour after your workout. This can help jumpstart the muscle-building process and support recovery.

Eat frequently: In order to support muscle growth, it's important to consume enough calories and nutrients throughout the day. Aim to eat 5-6 smaller meals throughout the day, rather than 2-3 large meals.

Plan ahead: Meal prepping can be a helpful strategy for ensuring you have healthy, muscle-building meals available when you need them. Plan out your meals and snacks in advance, and consider prepping food in bulk to save time and energy.

Avoid excessive alcohol consumption: Alcohol can interfere with muscle recovery and growth, so it's best to limit your consumption or avoid it altogether. If you do choose to drink, aim to do so in moderation and make sure to stay hydrated.

Listen to your body: Everyone's nutritional needs are different, and it's important to pay attention to how your body responds to different foods and eating patterns. If you find that certain foods or strategies aren't working for you, adjust your approach accordingly.

Remember, nutrition is just one piece of the puzzle when it comes to Heavy Duty Training. In addition to fueling your body properly, it's also important to get enough rest and recovery, and to focus on proper technique and form during your workouts. With a balanced approach, you can maximize your muscle-building potential and achieve your goals.

5 RECOVERY AND REST FOR HEAVY DUTY TRAINING

Heavy Duty Training is an intense form of resistance training that places a lot of stress on the body. As a result, proper recovery and rest are crucial to maximizing your results and avoiding injury.

Here are some tips for optimizing your recovery and rest:

Get enough sleep: Adequate sleep is essential for muscle recovery and growth. Aim to get 7-9 hours of sleep each night, and prioritize a consistent sleep schedule.

Take rest days: While Heavy Duty Training involves fewer workouts per week, those workouts are highly intense and demanding. Make sure to take at least one or two full rest days each week to allow your body to recover.

Foam roll and stretch: Foam rolling and stretching can help to alleviate muscle soreness and tightness, and promote blood flow and recovery. Make sure to incorporate these practices into your routine on a regular basis.

Listen to your body: If you feel excessively fatigued or experience pain or discomfort during your workouts, it may be a sign that your body needs more rest or recovery time. Pay attention to these signals and adjust your approach accordingly.

Incorporate active recovery: While rest days are important, it's also helpful to incorporate some low-intensity activity on those days. Activities like walking, swimming, or yoga can help to promote blood flow and recovery without adding additional stress to the body.

Use recovery tools: Tools like compression sleeves, ice packs, and massage balls can also be helpful for promoting recovery and reducing muscle soreness. Experiment with different tools and find what works best for you.

Remember, recovery and rest are just as important as your workouts when it comes to Heavy Duty Training. Prioritize adequate sleep, rest days, and recovery strategies to maximize your results and avoid injury.

Hydrate properly: Adequate hydration is essential for muscle recovery and overall health. Make sure to drink enough water throughout the day, particularly during and after your workouts.

Manage stress: High levels of stress can negatively impact recovery and muscle growth. Incorporate stress management techniques into your routine, such as meditation, deep breathing, or yoga.

Consider supplementation: While nutrition should always come first, certain supplements can be helpful for promoting recovery and muscle growth. Some popular options include protein powder, creatine, and branched-chain amino acids (BCAAs).

Give yourself time: Building muscle takes time, and it's important to be patient and consistent with your approach. Remember that progress is not always linear, and focus on making small improvements over time.

By prioritizing recovery and rest, you can maximize the benefits of Heavy Duty Training and achieve your muscle-building goals. Remember to listen to your body, be consistent with your approach, and prioritize self-care and recovery strategies.

Consider the role of nutrition: Proper nutrition is essential for recovery and muscle growth. Make sure to consume enough protein to support muscle repair and growth, and incorporate a variety of nutrient-dense foods into your diet.

Avoid overtraining: While Heavy Duty Training can be highly effective, it's important to avoid overtraining. Overtraining can lead to fatigue, injury, and decreased performance. Make sure to monitor your training volume and intensity, and adjust as needed to avoid overdoing it.

Use progressive overload: Progressive overload is the key to building muscle and strength over time. Make sure to gradually increase the weight and/or reps of your exercises over time to challenge your muscles and stimulate growth.

Keep a training log: Keeping a training log can be helpful for tracking your progress and monitoring your recovery. Make note of your workouts, including the exercises, sets, and reps you performed, as well as how you felt during and after the workout.

Be consistent: Consistency is key when it comes to Heavy Duty Training. Stick to a regular workout schedule, prioritize recovery and rest, and make sure to fuel your body properly with adequate nutrition and hydration.

By following these tips, you can optimize your recovery and rest and maximize the benefits of Heavy Duty Training. Remember to be patient, consistent, and prioritize self-care and recovery strategies to support your muscle-building goals.

6 EXERCISES FOR HEAVY DUTY TRAINING

Heavy Duty Training involves high-intensity workouts that focus on a few key exercises. Here are some of the most effective exercises for Heavy Duty Training:

Squats: Squats are a compound exercise that work multiple muscle groups, including the quads, hamstrings, glutes, and core. They are a highly effective exercise for building lower body strength and mass.

Deadlifts: Deadlifts are another compound exercise that work multiple muscle groups, including the back, glutes, and legs. They are one of the most effective exercises for building overall strength and power.

Bench Press: The bench press is a classic upper body exercise that works the chest, shoulders, and triceps. It is a highly effective exercise for building upper body strength and mass.

Rows: Rows are an effective exercise for building upper back strength and mass. They can be performed with a barbell, dumbbells, or a cable machine.

Pull-ups: Pull-ups are a challenging exercise that work the back, shoulders, and arms. They are an effective exercise for building upper body strength and muscle mass.

Overhead Press: The overhead press is an upper body exercise that targets the shoulders and triceps. It is an effective exercise for building upper body strength and mass.

Lunges: Lunges are a unilateral lower body exercise that work the quads, hamstrings, and glutes. They can be performed with bodyweight, dumbbells, or a barbell.

Dips: Dips are an effective exercise for building tricep strength and mass. They can be performed on parallel bars, dip machines, or with a bench.

Calf Raises: Calf raises are an effective exercise for building lower leg strength and mass. They can be performed with bodyweight, dumbbells, or a calf raise machine.

Abdominal Exercises: Abdominal exercises like planks, sit-ups, and crunches are important for building core strength and stability.

When performing these exercises for Heavy Duty Training, it's important to focus on proper form and technique. Start with lighter weights and gradually increase the weight and/or reps over time to challenge your muscles and stimulate growth. Remember to prioritize recovery and rest to support muscle repair and growth.

Barbell and Dumbbell Shrugs: Shrugs are an isolation exercise that target the trapezius muscles. They are performed by lifting the shoulders towards the ears and squeezing them at the top of the movement. They can be performed with a barbell or dumbbells.

Barbell and Dumbbell Curls: Curls are an isolation exercise that target the biceps. They can be performed with a barbell or dumbbells.

Triceps Extensions: Triceps extensions are an isolation exercise that target the triceps. They can be performed with a cable machine, dumbbells, or a barbell.

Leg Press: The leg press is a machine-based exercise that works the quads, hamstrings, and glutes. It is an effective exercise for building lower body strength and mass.

Chest Flyes: Chest flyes are an isolation exercise that target the chest muscles. They can be performed with dumbbells, a cable machine, or a fly machine.

Lateral Raises: Lateral raises are an isolation exercise that target the deltoid muscles. They can be performed with dumbbells or a cable machine.

Pull-Downs: Pull-downs are an exercise that work the back muscles, specifically the latissimus dorsi. They can be performed with a cable machine or a pull-down machine.

Hammer Curls: Hammer curls are an isolation exercise that target the brachialis and brachioradialis muscles in the forearm. They can be performed with dumbbells or a cable machine.

Leg Curls: Leg curls are an isolation exercise that target the hamstrings. They can be performed with a machine or with a resistance band.

Incline Press: Incline press is an upper body exercise that targets the upper chest muscles. It can be performed with a barbell or dumbbells.

By incorporating these exercises into your Heavy Duty Training routine, you can effectively target and stimulate all major muscle groups. Remember to focus on proper form and technique, gradually increase weight and/or reps over time, and prioritize recovery and rest to support muscle growth and development.

When designing a Heavy Duty Training program, it's important to select exercises that will effectively target all major muscle groups while minimizing the risk of injury. The exercises listed in this chapter have been chosen based on their effectiveness for building muscle mass and strength, as well as their relative safety and ease of execution.

It's worth noting that some of these exercises may be more challenging to perform than others, particularly if you're new to strength training. For example, exercises like deadlifts and squats require proper form and technique to avoid injury, so it's important to seek guidance from a qualified trainer or coach if you're not familiar with these exercises.

In addition to selecting the right exercises, it's important to incorporate the appropriate amount of weight and reps into your Heavy Duty Training program. The goal should be to lift heavy enough weights to stimulate muscle growth, while also allowing for adequate recovery time between workouts.

As you progress in your training, you may need to gradually increase the amount of weight or reps you're lifting to continue seeing progress. This can be done by increasing the weight you're lifting by small increments each week or by performing more reps with the same weight.

Ultimately, the key to success with Heavy Duty Training is to prioritize consistency and dedication in your workouts, while also listening to your body and adjusting your routine as needed to support optimal progress and results.

7 NUTRITION FOR HEAVY DUTY TRAINING (ADVANCED)

When it comes to building muscle and strength, proper nutrition is just as important as your training program. To support muscle growth and development, it's important to eat a balanced diet that provides your body with the nutrients it needs to repair and rebuild muscle tissue.

Here are some key nutrition tips to keep in mind when following a Heavy Duty Training program:

Eat Enough Calories: Building muscle requires a calorie surplus, which means you need to consume more calories than your body burns on a daily basis. Aim to consume 250-500 calories more than your maintenance level each day to support muscle growth.

Prioritize Protein: Protein is essential for muscle growth and repair. Aim to consume 1 gram of protein per pound of bodyweight each day, and include protein-rich foods like chicken, fish, lean beef, eggs, and plant-based sources like beans and tofu in your diet.

Carbs for Energy: Carbohydrates provide energy for your workouts and support muscle recovery. Include complex carbs like whole grains, fruits, and vegetables in your diet to fuel your workouts and support muscle growth.

Don't Forget About Healthy Fats: Healthy fats like those found in nuts, seeds, avocado, and fatty fish are important for overall health and hormone regulation, which can impact muscle growth and recovery.

Hydrate: Adequate hydration is essential for muscle function and recovery. Aim to consume at least 8-10 cups of water per day, and more if you're training intensely or in hot weather.

Timing Matters: Eating before and after your workouts can help support muscle growth and recovery. Aim to eat a balanced meal with protein and carbs within an hour of finishing your workout, and consider a pre-workout snack to fuel your session.

Supplements Can Help: While not essential, certain supplements like whey protein, creatine, and beta-alanine can help support muscle growth and improve performance. Consult with a healthcare professional before starting any supplement regimen.

By following these nutrition tips, you can support your Heavy Duty Training program and maximize your muscle-building potential. Remember that nutrition is a key component of any fitness program, and by eating a balanced diet that supports your goals, you can see the results you're after.

In addition to these general nutrition tips, there are some specific dietary strategies that can be especially beneficial for those following a Heavy Duty Training program.

Prioritize Post-Workout Nutrition: Consuming a meal or snack within an hour of finishing your workout can help promote muscle recovery and growth. Aim for a balanced meal that includes protein and carbohydrates to refuel your body and support muscle repair.

Consider a High-Protein Diet: Some studies suggest that a high-protein diet may be especially beneficial for building muscle. Aim to consume at least 1 gram of protein per pound of bodyweight each day, and consider adding protein-rich snacks like Greek yogurt or protein bars to your diet to meet your protein needs.

Timing Your Carb Intake: Carbohydrates provide energy for your workouts, so it can be helpful to time your carb intake around your training sessions. Consuming carbs before your workout can help provide energy for your session, while consuming carbs after your workout can help replenish glycogen stores and support muscle recovery.

Focus on Whole Foods: While supplements can be helpful, it's important to prioritize whole foods in your diet to provide your body with the nutrients it needs to support muscle growth and overall health. Focus on whole, nutrient-dense foods like fruits, vegetables, lean proteins, and whole grains.

Stay Hydrated: Adequate hydration is important for muscle function and recovery. Aim to consume at least 8-10 cups of water per day, and more if you're training intensely or in hot weather.

Remember that nutrition is an individualized aspect of fitness, and what works for one person may not work for another. It's important to experiment with different dietary strategies to find what works best for your body and your goals. Consulting with a registered dietitian or certified nutritionist can also be helpful in developing a nutrition plan that's tailored to your needs and goals.

In addition to the dietary strategies mentioned above, there are also some supplements that may be helpful for those following a Heavy Duty Training program. Here are some of the most commonly recommended supplements:

Whey Protein: Whey protein is a fast-digesting protein source that can be helpful for promoting muscle recovery and growth. Consuming whey protein powder before or after your workout can help provide your body with the amino acids it needs to repair and build muscle tissue.

Creatine: Creatine is a natural compound that helps provide energy for high-intensity exercise. Taking creatine supplements can help increase muscle strength and size, as well as improve exercise performance.

Beta-Alanine: Beta-alanine is an amino acid that helps buffer lactic acid in the muscles, which can help delay fatigue during intense exercise. Taking beta-alanine supplements can help improve endurance and performance during high-intensity training sessions.

Branched-Chain Amino Acids (BCAAs): BCAAs are a group of amino acids that are especially important for muscle recovery and growth. Consuming BCAAs during or after your workout can help support muscle repair and growth.

Fish Oil: Fish oil supplements are a rich source of omega-3 fatty acids, which have been shown to have numerous health benefits, including reducing inflammation and improving heart health. Taking fish oil supplements can also help support muscle recovery and growth.

While these supplements can be helpful, it's important to remember that they're not a replacement for a healthy diet and consistent training program.

Always consult with a healthcare professional before starting any new supplement regimen.

8 RECOVERY AND REST (ADVANCED)

Rest and recovery are essential components of any effective training program, and this is especially true for those following a Heavy Duty Training program. Here are some key strategies for maximizing your recovery and rest:

Sleep: Getting enough sleep is crucial for muscle recovery and growth. Aim for at least 7-9 hours of sleep each night, and prioritize good sleep hygiene practices like avoiding electronics before bed and keeping your bedroom dark and cool.

Active Recovery: While taking a day off from training is important, it can also be helpful to engage in low-intensity activities like yoga or walking on your off days. These activities can help promote blood flow to your muscles and support muscle recovery.

Stretching and Foam Rolling: Stretching and foam rolling can help reduce muscle soreness and improve flexibility, which can in turn support muscle recovery and growth. Aim to stretch or foam roll for at least 10-15 minutes after each workout.

Massage: Massage can be a helpful tool for promoting muscle recovery and reducing muscle tension. Consider getting a professional massage or using a foam roller or massage gun to target sore or tight muscles.

Proper Nutrition: As mentioned earlier, nutrition plays a key role in muscle recovery and growth. Make sure you're consuming enough protein, carbohydrates, and other nutrients to support your body's recovery needs.

Remember that everyone's recovery needs are different, and it's important to listen to your body and adjust your recovery strategies as needed. If you're experiencing persistent muscle soreness, fatigue, or other signs of overtraining, it may be time to take a break or adjust your training program. Always consult with a healthcare professional if you have concerns about your recovery or rest strategies.

Another important aspect of recovery and rest is managing stress. High levels of stress can interfere with muscle recovery and growth, so it's important to prioritize stress management strategies like meditation, deep breathing, or other relaxation techniques. Additionally, it's important to avoid overtraining and give your body adequate time to recover between workouts. This may mean adjusting your workout frequency, intensity, or duration as needed.

Finally, it's important to stay consistent with your recovery and rest strategies. Don't skimp on sleep or skip your stretching routine just because you're feeling pressed for time. Making rest and recovery a priority can help you avoid injury, prevent burnout, and make consistent progress towards your muscle-building goals.

Overall, while the Heavy Duty Training program emphasizes intense, low-volume workouts, it's important to remember that recovery and rest are just as important as the workout itself. By prioritizing good sleep, active recovery, stretching, massage, nutrition, stress management, and consistency, you can optimize your recovery and support your body's muscle-building efforts.

When it comes to recovery and rest, it's important to understand that there is no one-size-fits-all approach. Recovery needs can vary depending on factors like age, training history, and overall health status. For example, older individuals may require more recovery time than younger individuals, and those with certain medical conditions may need to modify their recovery strategies accordingly.

Additionally, recovery needs may vary depending on the type of workout you're doing. For example, a high-intensity, heavy lifting session may require more recovery time than a low-intensity cardio session. It's important to pay attention to your body's signals and adjust your recovery strategies accordingly.

Another important aspect of recovery and rest is hydration. Drinking enough water can help support muscle recovery and prevent dehydration, which can negatively impact muscle function and recovery. Aim to drink at least 8-10 glasses of water each day, and consider drinking an electrolyte drink or consuming a post-workout protein shake to support hydration and muscle recovery.

Finally, it's worth noting that overtraining is a real risk for those following a Heavy Duty Training program. Overtraining can lead to muscle fatigue, injury, and burnout, and can even hinder muscle growth over time. To avoid overtraining, make sure you're giving your body enough time to rest and recover between workouts, and consider incorporating deload weeks into your training program. Deload weeks involve reducing the intensity or volume of your workouts to allow your body to recover fully.

Overall, effective recovery and rest strategies are essential for optimizing muscle growth and preventing injury and burnout. By paying attention to your body's signals, staying consistent with recovery strategies, and avoiding overtraining, you can support your body's muscle-building efforts and make consistent progress towards your fitness goals.

9 COMMON MISTAKES TO AVOID IN HEAVY DUTY TRAINING

While the Heavy Duty Training program can be an effective approach to building muscle and strength, there are some common mistakes that individuals may make when following this type of program. Here are a few mistakes to avoid:

Neglecting Proper Form: Proper form is essential when lifting heavy weights. Improper form can lead to injury and prevent you from making progress towards your goals. Make sure to learn proper form for each exercise and focus on maintaining good form throughout your workouts.

Not Warming Up Properly: Warming up is important to prevent injury and prepare your body for your workout. Skipping your warm-up or not warming up properly can increase your risk of injury and limit your ability to perform your best during your workout.

Not Tracking Progress: Progress tracking is important to ensure that you're making progress towards your goals. If you're not tracking your workouts and progress, it can be difficult to know if you're making progress or need to adjust your training program.

Overtraining: Overtraining can lead to injury, burnout, and hinder muscle growth. Make sure to give your body enough time to rest and recover between workouts and avoid working the same muscle groups too frequently.

Not Getting Enough Sleep: Sleep is essential for muscle recovery and growth. Not getting enough sleep can negatively impact your muscle-building efforts and increase your risk of injury and burnout.

Not Prioritizing Nutrition: Nutrition is important to support muscle recovery and growth. Make sure to eat a well-balanced diet with enough protein, carbohydrates, and healthy fats to support your muscle-building efforts.

Ignoring Pain or Injury: Pain or injury should never be ignored. If you're experiencing pain or discomfort during your workouts, it's important to address it and seek medical attention if necessary.

Overall, by avoiding these common mistakes, you can optimize your Heavy Duty Training program and make consistent progress towards your muscle-building goals.

In addition to the common mistakes mentioned above, there are a few other important things to keep in mind when following a Heavy Duty Training program. Here are a few additional tips:

Focus on Compound Movements: Compound exercises such as squats, deadlifts, bench press, and overhead press should be the cornerstone of your training program. These exercises work multiple muscle groups at once and allow you to lift heavy weights, which can help stimulate muscle growth.

Use Proper Breathing Techniques: Proper breathing is important when lifting heavy weights. Make sure to exhale during the concentric (lifting) phase and inhale during the eccentric (lowering) phase of the exercise. This can help improve your performance and prevent injury.

Gradually Increase Intensity: While Heavy Duty Training involves lifting heavy weights, it's important to gradually increase the intensity of your workouts. If you start with weights that are too heavy, you increase your risk of injury and hinder your ability to make progress towards your goals.

Listen to Your Body: It's important to listen to your body and adjust your training program as needed. If you're feeling fatigued or experiencing pain or discomfort, it may be time to take a break or adjust your training program.

By following these tips and avoiding common mistakes, you can optimize your Heavy Duty Training program and achieve your muscle-building goals more effectively. Remember to always prioritize proper form, rest and recovery, nutrition, and gradual progression to ensure long-term success.

10 FINAL THOUGHTS AND CONCLUSION

In this book, we've explored the Heavy Duty Training method, which is based on the principles of high intensity, low volume, and infrequent training. We've looked at the history of the method, its benefits, and some common mistakes to avoid.

It's important to note that Heavy Duty Training may not be suitable for everyone. Beginners and those with injuries or health conditions should consult with a medical professional before starting a new exercise program. Additionally, Heavy Duty Training requires a significant amount of focus and intensity, which may not be sustainable for everyone in the long term.

However, for those who are able to effectively implement the Heavy Duty Training method, it can be a highly effective way to build muscle and increase strength. By following the principles of Heavy Duty Training, including lifting heavy weights with proper form, prioritizing recovery, and gradually increasing intensity, you can achieve your muscle-building goals more efficiently.

Ultimately, the key to success with any training program is consistency, dedication, and a willingness to adapt and make changes as needed. By incorporating the principles of Heavy Duty Training into your overall fitness routine, you can take your muscle-building efforts to the next level and achieve your desired physique.

In addition to the key takeaways of the book, there are a few more things to consider in the final chapter.

First, it's important to remember that Heavy Duty Training is just one approach to building muscle and increasing strength. There are many other training methods and styles out there, and what works best for one person may not work as well for another. Experimenting with different training styles and finding what works best for your body is an important part of the fitness journey.

Second, it's important to emphasize the importance of nutrition and rest when it comes to building muscle. Heavy Duty Training can be physically and mentally demanding, and proper nutrition and rest are essential for recovery and muscle growth. Make sure to eat a balanced diet that includes plenty of protein, healthy fats, and complex carbohydrates, and prioritize getting enough sleep and rest to allow your body to recover.

Finally, it's worth noting that building muscle and increasing strength takes time and consistency. While Heavy Duty Training can help accelerate your progress, it's important to have realistic expectations and not get discouraged if you don't see immediate results. Consistency and dedication to your training and nutrition are key to achieving your goals.

Overall, the Heavy Duty Training method can be a highly effective way to build muscle and increase strength, but it's important to approach it with a focus on proper form, recovery, and gradual progression. By incorporating the principles of Heavy Duty Training into your overall fitness routine and staying committed to your goals, you can achieve the results you're looking for.

To ensure success with Heavy Duty Training, it's important to prioritize form and technique when performing each exercise. This means using proper form to target the intended muscle group, avoiding cheating or momentum, and using a controlled tempo. It's also important to choose exercises that are appropriate for your skill level and goals.

Another key aspect of Heavy Duty Training is recovery. With high intensity and low volume, your muscles will need more time to recover and grow. This means incorporating rest days into your training schedule, getting enough sleep and rest, and ensuring proper nutrition. Overtraining can be counterproductive and may lead to injury or burnout, so it's important to find a balance that works for you.

Gradual progression is also important in Heavy Duty Training. As you become stronger and more experienced, it's important to increase the weight, reps, or intensity of your exercises gradually. This will challenge your muscles and help promote growth, but be careful not to increase too much too quickly and risk injury.

Finally, it's important to stay motivated and committed to your goals. Building muscle and increasing strength takes time and dedication, and it's important to stay consistent even when progress may seem slow. Tracking your progress, setting achievable goals, and finding a workout partner or community can all help keep you motivated and on track.

In conclusion, the Heavy Duty Training method can be a highly effective way to build muscle and increase strength, but it's important to approach it with a focus on proper form, recovery, and gradual progression. By incorporating the principles of Heavy Duty Training into your overall fitness routine and staying committed to your goals, you can achieve the results you're looking for.

To achieve optimal results with Heavy Duty Training, it's important to understand the importance of proper nutrition. Building muscle requires a sufficient intake of calories and macronutrients such as protein, carbohydrates, and healthy fats. It's important to fuel your body with nutrient-dense foods such as lean proteins, complex carbohydrates, and vegetables, while minimizing processed and junk foods.

Timing your meals and snacks around your workouts can also be beneficial for muscle growth and recovery. Eating a balanced meal containing protein and carbohydrates within 30 minutes to an hour after your workout can help refuel your muscles and promote recovery. It's also important to stay hydrated by drinking plenty of water throughout the day.

Supplements can also play a role in supporting muscle growth and recovery, but they should not be relied upon as a substitute for proper nutrition. Some popular supplements for muscle growth include whey protein, creatine, and beta-alanine. It's important to do your research and consult with a healthcare professional before starting any new supplements.

Additionally, managing stress levels and getting enough rest and recovery time is important for overall health and fitness. Stress can have negative effects on muscle growth and recovery, so finding ways to manage stress such as meditation or yoga can be beneficial. Getting enough sleep is also important for muscle growth and recovery, as this is when the body repairs and rebuilds muscle tissue.

By taking a holistic approach to fitness and incorporating proper nutrition, stress management, and recovery into your Heavy Duty Training routine, you can optimize your results and achieve your muscle-building goals.

In addition to proper nutrition, there are several other factors that can impact muscle growth and recovery when following a Heavy Duty Training program.

Firstly, it's important to gradually increase the intensity and volume of your workouts over time. Starting with a lower intensity and gradually increasing the weight and reps can help prevent injury and improve muscle growth. It's also important to vary your workouts and incorporate a variety of exercises to target different muscle groups and prevent boredom.

Proper form is also crucial for preventing injury and maximizing muscle activation during your workouts. It's important to focus on proper technique and use weights that you can handle with good form. Working with a qualified trainer or coach can be helpful in learning proper form and technique.

Rest and recovery are also important for muscle growth and preventing injury. Taking rest days and incorporating active recovery such as stretching and foam rolling can help prevent muscle soreness and improve overall performance. Overtraining can lead to injury and hinder muscle growth, so it's important to listen to your body and take adequate rest when needed.

Lastly, having a strong mindset and setting realistic goals can also play a role in achieving success with Heavy Duty Training. Staying motivated and committed to your training can be challenging, so finding ways to stay inspired and setting achievable goals can help you stay on track and achieve your desired results.

Another important factor to consider when following a Heavy Duty Training program is the importance of proper sleep and recovery. Getting enough sleep is crucial for muscle growth and repair, as well as overall health and well-being. During sleep, the body releases growth hormone, which helps stimulate muscle growth and repair. Aim for at least 7-8 hours of sleep per night, and try to establish a consistent sleep schedule to help improve sleep quality.

In addition to sleep, nutrition is also critical for muscle growth and recovery. Following a diet that is rich in protein, healthy fats, and complex carbohydrates can provide the nutrients needed to fuel workouts and support muscle growth. It's also important to stay hydrated and drink plenty of water throughout the day.

Supplements can also be a helpful addition to a Heavy Duty Training program, but they should be used in conjunction with a healthy diet and proper training. Some supplements that may be beneficial for muscle growth and recovery include protein powder, creatine, and branched-chain amino acids (BCAAs).

Proper warm-up and cool-down routines are also important for preventing injury and optimizing performance during Heavy Duty Training. A dynamic warm-up that incorporates stretching and mobility exercises can help prepare the muscles and joints for exercise, while a cool-down that includes static stretching and foam rolling can help improve flexibility and reduce muscle soreness.

Lastly, it's important to listen to your body and adjust your training as needed. While Heavy Duty Training can be an effective approach for muscle growth, it may not be suitable for everyone. If you experience pain or discomfort during your workouts, it may be necessary to adjust the weight or intensity, or take a break from training altogether. It's important to prioritize safety and injury prevention when following any training program.

Mike Mentzer was a strong advocate of the Heavy Duty Training philosophy and believed in its effectiveness for building muscle mass and strength. He stressed the importance of intensity and effort in each workout, and emphasized the need for proper recovery in between sessions.

Mentzer believed that overtraining was a common problem in the bodybuilding community and that many individuals were not giving their muscles enough time to recover and grow. He argued that a Heavy Duty Training program could be more effective than traditional training methods because it focused on high-intensity workouts performed less frequently, which allowed for adequate recovery time.

Mentzer also emphasized the importance of proper form and technique during exercises, as well as the need for variety in training routines to prevent plateaus and keep the muscles challenged. He believed that focusing on a small number of compound exercises that target multiple muscle groups, such as squats, deadlifts, and bench presses, was more effective than performing a large number of isolation exercises.

In addition to his training philosophy, Mentzer also emphasized the importance of nutrition and recovery in building muscle mass. He recommended consuming a high-protein diet and staying hydrated, and stressed the need for adequate rest and recovery between workouts. Mentzer also believed in the importance of mental focus and concentration during workouts, and encouraged individuals to push themselves to their limits during each session.

Overall, Mentzer's thoughts on Heavy Duty Training focused on the need for intensity, proper form and technique, and adequate recovery to promote muscle growth and strength. By following these principles and focusing on a small number of high-intensity exercises, individuals can achieve impressive results in their training and build the physique they desire.

In addition to Mike Mentzer's thoughts on Heavy Duty Training, it's important to understand the specific principles that underpin this approach to weight training.

Firstly, Heavy Duty Training emphasizes the importance of intensity and effort in each workout. This means pushing yourself to your limits during each set, with the goal of achieving momentary muscular failure. By doing so, you stimulate muscle growth and strength gains, while avoiding the risk of overtraining or injury.

Another key principle of Heavy Duty Training is the focus on compound exercises, which work multiple muscle groups simultaneously. Examples of compound exercises include squats, deadlifts, bench presses, and pull-ups. These exercises are typically performed with heavier weights and lower reps than isolation exercises, which target specific muscles in isolation.

In addition to compound exercises, Heavy Duty Training emphasizes the importance of progressive overload. This means gradually increasing the weight or resistance used in your workouts over time, in order to challenge your muscles and encourage continued growth and development.

Recovery is also a crucial aspect of Heavy Duty Training. Because you're working your muscles to the point of momentary muscular failure, it's important to give your body time to rest and recover between workouts. This typically means training no more than two or three times per week, and allowing for at least one or two days of rest in between each session.

Finally, nutrition is a key component of Heavy Duty Training. To build muscle mass and strength, you need to consume enough calories and protein to support muscle growth and repair. This typically means eating a high-protein diet that includes plenty of lean meats, fish, eggs, and dairy products, as well as fruits, vegetables, and complex carbohydrates.

Overall, Heavy Duty Training is a challenging but effective approach to weight training that can help you build muscle mass, strength, and overall fitness. By focusing on intensity, compound exercises, progressive overload, recovery, and nutrition, you can achieve impressive results and develop the physique you desire.

ABOUT THE AUTHOR

As an author of a book on heavy duty training, I have established myself as a knowledgeable and experienced fitness expert. My book provides a comprehensive guide for anyone looking to develop strength, endurance, and muscle mass through rigorous and effective training.

My passion for fitness is evident in my writing, and readers can feel my enthusiasm for heavy duty training jump off the page. I have a deep understanding of the science behind building muscle, and I am able to communicate complex concepts in a clear and concise manner, making my book accessible to beginners and experienced athletes alike.

My approach to heavy duty training is grounded in research and practical experience. I understand that a one-size-fits-all approach does not work for everyone, and I provide readers with a range of options for customizing their workouts to meet their individual needs and goals. Whether someone is looking to bulk up, increase their endurance, or simply improve their overall fitness, my book offers a wealth of information and practical advice to help them achieve their goals.

As an author, I am dedicated to helping my readers reach their full potential and achieve their fitness goals through effective and science-based training. I am excited to share my knowledge and expertise with the world, and I believe that my book on heavy duty training will be a valuable resource for anyone looking to take their fitness to the next level.

Made in United States
Troutdale, OR
08/14/2023

12076700R00030